Connect

SECOND EDITION

Jack C. Richards
Carlos Barbisan
with Chuck Sandy
and Dorothy E. Zemach

Workbook 1

CAMBRIDGE
UNIVERSITY PRESS

CAMBRIDGE
UNIVERSITY PRESS

University Printing House, Cambridge CB2 8BS, United Kingdom

One Liberty Plaza, 20th Floor, New York, NY 10006, USA

477 Williamstown Road, Port Melbourne, VIC 3207, Australia

314–321, 3rd Floor, Plot 3, Splendor Forum, Jasola District Centre, New Delhi – 110025, India

103 Penang Road, #05-06/07, Visioncrest Commercial, Singapore 238467

Cambridge University Press is part of the University of Cambridge.

It furthers the University's mission by disseminating knowledge in the pursuit of
education, learning and research at the highest international levels of excellence.

www.cambridge.org
Information on this title: www.cambridge.org/9780521736985

© Cambridge University Press 2009

This publication is in copyright. Subject to statutory exception
and to the provisions of relevant collective licensing agreements,
no reproduction of any part may take place without the written
permission of Cambridge University Press.

First published 2004
Second edition 2009

40 39 38 37

Printed in Malaysia by Vivar Printing

A catalog record for this publication is available from the British Library

ISBN 978-0-521-73694-7 Student's Book 1 (English)
ISBN 978-0-521-73695-4 Student's Book 1 (Portuguese)
ISBN 978-0-521-73698-5 Workbook 1 (English)
ISBN 978-0-521-73699-2 Workbook 1 (Portuguese)
ISBN 978-0-521-73700-5 Teacher's Edition 1 (English)
ISBN 978-0-521-73701-2 Teacher's Edition 1 (Portuguese)
ISBN 978-0-521-73697-8 Class Audio CDs

Cambridge University Press has no responsibility for the persistence or accuracy
of URLs for external or third-party internet websites referred to in this publication,
and does not guarantee that any content on such websites is, or will remain,
accurate or appropriate.

Art direction, photo research, and layout services: A+ comunicação
Book design: Adventure House, NYC

Table of Contents

Classmates

1 **Number the sentences in the correct order.**

_____ Nice to meet you, Ana.

_____ My name is Ana.

_1_ Hi. I'm Valerie. What's your name?

_____ Nice to meet you, too.

2 **Choose the correct words to complete the conversation.**

A Hello. My name is Koji.
What's (Is / What's) your name?

B Hi, Koji. _____ (I'm / My) Joanie.
Nice to meet you.

A Nice to meet _____ (you / your), too.

3 **Introduce yourself to Jake. Complete the conversation.**

Hi. My name is Jake. What's your name?

_____

Nice to meet you.

_____

UNIT 1 Back to School

1 **Look at the pictures. Complete the conversations with the sentences in the box.**

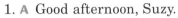

☐ Fine, thank you.   ☐ Good morning.   ☑ How are you today?
☐ Good evening.   ☐ How about you?   ☐ Not too good.

1. **A** Good afternoon, Suzy.
   B *How are you today?*
   A _____
   B Great!

2. **A** _____
   How are you?
   B Not bad, thanks.
   _____
   A Good.

3. **A** _____
   B Hello, Mr. Gomez. How are you?
   A _____

2 **Choose the correct titles.**

1. I'm ___*Miss*___ (Miss / Mrs.) Johnson.
   I'm single.

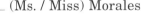

2. My name is _____ (Ms. / Miss) Morales.
   I'm married.

3. I'm _____ (Mrs. / Mr.) Weston.
   I'm married.

4. My name is _____ (Mrs. / Ms.) Lee.
   I'm single.

1 Complete the conversations with the words in the box.

☐ are   ☑ hi   ☐ meet   ☐ nice   ☐ thanks
☐ hello   ☐ how   ☐ my   ☐ not   ☐ your

1. **A** _Hi_ . I'm Eva. What's _____ name?

   B _____ name is Matt.

   A _____ to meet you, Matt.

   B Nice to _____ you, too.

2. **A** Hi, Miss Valdes.

   B _____ , Corey. How _____ you today?

   A _____ bad. _____ about you?

   B Great, _____ .

2 Rewrite the sentences. Correct the underlined words.

1. <u>Bad</u> to meet you, Lydia.

   Nice to meet you, Lydia.

2. Hi. I'm Mrs. Martinez. What's your <u>afternoon</u>?

   _____

3. Hi. My <u>hello</u> is Robert.

   _____

4. <u>What's</u> are you today?

   _____

5. I'm not bad. How about <u>your</u>?

   _____

6. <u>OK</u> afternoon, Mrs. Lyon.

   _____

7. <u>Good</u> I'm late, Mr. Morgan.

   _____

1 Choose the correct words to complete the conversations.

1. **A** _Hi_ (Hi / Bye), Carla.

   B Hello, Rose. This _____ (is / are) Doug Jones.

   A Nice to _____ (see / meet) you, Doug.

2. **A** _____ (Good-bye / Hello), Tom.

   B See you _____ (late / later), Mr. Shields.

3. **A** _____ (Good-bye / Good evening), Ms. Cooper. How are you?

   B I'm good, _____ (thank / thanks).

4. **A** Sarah, _____ (you / this) is Ms. Nelson.

   Ms. Nelson, _____ (you / this) is Sarah Finnegan.

   B Nice to meet _____ (you / your), Ms. Nelson.

   C Nice to meet you, _____ (you / too), Sarah.

2 Match the pictures to the conversations in Part 1.

a.

b.

c.

d.

3 Write the correct responses.

1. Gisele, this is Pedro.

   _____

2. Nice to meet you.

   _____

3. How are you today?

   _____

4. See you tomorrow.

   _____

1 **Look at the pictures. Complete the forms for the students.**

1.
   First Name: *Leticia*
   Last Name: *Webber*

2. **First Name:**
   Last Name:

3. **First Name:**
   Last Name:

4.
   First Name:
   Last Name:

2 **Match the questions to the answers.**

1. Hello. How are you today? __d__
2. What's your name? ____
3. How do you spell your first name? ____
4. And how do you spell your last name? ____

a. Leticia Webber.
b. L-E-T-I-C-I-A.
c. W-E-B-B-E-R.
d. Good, thanks.

3 **Complete the conversation in Part 2 with your own information.**

A *Hello. How are you today?* _____

You _____

A *What's your name?* _____

You _____

A _____

You _____

A _____

You _____

Get Connected
UNIT 1

1 Read the conversation quickly. Write the first names of the two people.

1. _____   2. _____

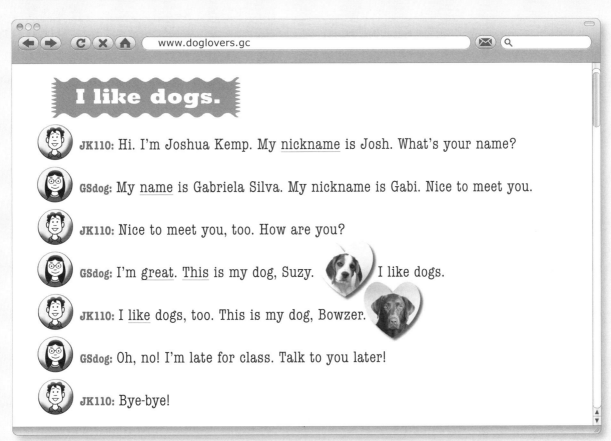

www.doglovers.gc

I like dogs.

JK110: Hi. I'm Joshua Kemp. My <u>nickname</u> is Josh. What's your name?

GSdog: My <u>name</u> is Gabriela Silva. My nickname is Gabi. Nice to meet you.

JK110: Nice to meet you, too. How are you?

GSdog: I'm <u>great</u>. <u>This</u> is my dog, Suzy.   I like dogs.

JK110: I <u>like</u> dogs, too. This is my dog, Bowzer.

GSdog: Oh, no! I'm late for class. Talk to you later!

JK110: Bye-bye!

2 Complete the sentences. Use the underlined words in the conversation in Part 1.

1. My first name is Madison. My
   _nickname_____ is Maddy.
2. I _____ music.
3. _____ is my dog, Lucky.
4. My last _____ is Levinson.
5. I'm _____. How are you?

3 Read the conversation in Part 1 slowly. Complete the chart.

First name	Last name	Nickname	Dog's name
	Kemp		
		Gabi	

1 **Label the pictures with the sentences in the box.**

☐ Good afternoon. ☐ Good evening. ☐ Good morning. ☐ Good night.

1. _____

2. _____

3. _____

4. _____

2 **Match the sentences to the correct responses.**

1. How are you today? _____
2. How do you spell your name? _____
3. Nice to meet you. _____
4. Good afternoon, Mrs. Chu. _____
5. See you later, Mr. Simon. _____
6. My name is Grace. _____

a. B-R-Y-A-N.
b. Hi, Jasmine.
c. Good-bye, Pete.
d. Hi. My name is Diego.
e. Fine, thanks. How about you?
f. Nice to meet you, too.

3 **Complete the conversations.**

1. **Janet**   Hi! _____ name is Janet. What's _____ name?

   Sandy   _____ Sandy. Nice to meet _____ .

2.   **Lisa**   _____ are you today, Mrs. Martinez?

   Mrs. Martinez   Not _____ , thank you. How _____ you?

         Lisa   I'm great.

3. **Mr. Cohen**   _____ morning, Taro.

   Taro   _____ I'm late, Mr. Cohen.

Teachers and friends

UNIT 2 Favorite People

1 Who are the people in Cindy's life? Write two sentences for each number.

1. This is my computer partner.
   His name is Jack.

   This is my computer partner, Jack.

   Jack is my computer partner.

2. This is my best friend.
   Her name is Laura.

   _____

   _____

3. This is my math teacher.
   His name is Mr. Larson.

   _____

   _____

4. This is my classmate.
   Her name is Maggie.

   _____

   _____

2 Complete the conversations with *What's his name?*, *What's her name?*, or *Who's this?*

1. A _____Who's this?_____
   B My classmate.

2. A _____
   B Her name is Emily.

3. A _____
   B This is my friend, Larry.

4. A _____
   B His name is Mr. Fuller.

5. A _____
   B My coach.

6. A _____
   B Her name is Ms. Patterson.

Favorite stars

1 Complete the chart with the words in the box.

> ☑ actor   ☐ cartoon character   ☐ English teacher   ☐ singer
> ☐ basketball coach   ☐ classmate   ☐ model   ☐ TV star
> ☐ best friend   ☐ computer partner

People at school	Stars
	actor

2 Match the pictures to the sentences. Then write sentences with the words from the Stars column in Part 1.

1.

   a. This is Josh Hartnett.
   He's my favorite actor.

2.

   b. This is Gru.

   _____

3.  _a_

   c. This is Ryan Seacrest.

   _____

4.

   d. This is Tyson Beckford.

   _____

5.

   e. This is Alicia Keys.

   _____

Mini-review

1 Choose the correct responses.

1.

A What's her name?

B *Her name is Dina.*

☐ I'm Lisa.

☑ Her name is Dina.

2.

A Who's this?

B _____

☐ His English teacher is Mrs. Kramer.

☐ My best friend.

3.

A Who's your favorite actor?

B _____

☐ Johnny Depp.

☐ He's my classmate.

4.

A What's her name?

B _____

☐ Her name is Jenny.

☐ She's my tennis partner.

2 Complete the questions with the words in the box. Then answer the questions with your own information.

☐ best	☑ English	☐ last	☐ TV

1. **Q:** Who's your *English* teacher?

   A: _____

2. **Q:** Who's your favorite _____ star?

   A: _____

3. **Q:** What's your _____ name?

   A: _____

4. **Q:** Who's your _____ friend?

   A: _____

3 Who are your favorite stars? Complete the chart with your own information.

Star	Name	Sentence
1. model	*Gisele Bündchen*	*She's my favorite model.*
2. singer		
3. TV star		
4. actor		
5. cartoon character		

Birthdays

1 **Write the numbers.**

1. (7) _____seven_____   5. (12) _____   9. (4) _____

2. (18) _____   6. (3) _____   10. (16) _____

3. (20) _____   7. (19) _____   11. (8) _____

4. (6) _____   8. (11) _____   12. (1) _____

2 **Circle the correct words to complete the conversation.**

A Hi. My name's Carlos.

B (Good night / Hello). My name's John.

A (How / What) old (is / are) you?

B (You're / I'm) thirteen.

A (Who / How) about (your / my) little
    sister? (Is / Are) she six?

B (She's / He's) not (five / six).
    (She's / He's) four.

3 **Write questions. Use the information in the chart.**

	Louisa	Jeff	Keiko	Pedro
11	☑	☐	☐	☐
12	☐	☐	☐	☑
13	☐	☐	☑	☐
14	☐	☑	☐	☐

1. **Q:** _How old is Jeff?_
   A: He's fourteen.

2. **Q:** _____
   A: She's eleven.

3. **Q:** _____
   A: He's twelve.

4. **Q:** _____
   A: She's thirteen.

4 **Correct the sentences. Use the information in the chart in Part 3.**

1. Pedro is eleven.
   Pedro is twelve.

2. Jeff is twelve.
   _____

3. Louisa is seventeen.
   _____

4. Keiko is ten.
   _____

1 Match the questions to the answers.

1. Where are you from? ____
2. Where's John from? ____
3. Marisa's from Peru, right? ____
4. You're from Japan, right? ____
5. Where's she from? ____
6. He's from Portugal, right? ____

a. She's not from Peru. She's from Colombia.
b. I'm from Mexico.
c. I'm not from Japan. I'm from China.
d. He's from France.
e. He's not from Portugal. He's from Canada.
f. She's from the U.S.

2 Write questions and answers.

1. she? / Australia

   A _Where's she from?_
   B _She's from Australia._

2. he? / Colombia

   A _____
   B _____

3. she from Mexico, right? / from Brazil

   A _____
   B _____

4. he from Canada, right? / from the U.S.

   A _____
   B _____

5. you? / Brazil

   A _____
   B _____

6. she? / Venezuela

   A _____
   B _____

7. you from Peru, right? / from Colombia

   A _____
   B _____

8. he? / Portugal

   A _____
   B _____

1 **Read the article quickly. Underline the names and nicknames of the coach and the best friend.**

My Coach and My Friend

This is my basketball coach, Ms. Rider. She's my science teacher, too. Her nickname is Coach R. Her favorite sports are basketball, soccer, and tennis. She's not from the U.S. She's from Canada. I think she's really funny. She's my favorite teacher. And she's my favorite coach, too!

Here's a photo of my best friend, Rafael. His nickname is Rafi. He's not from the U.S. He's from Peru. His favorite TV show is *Heroes*. His favorite TV star is Mario Lopez. He likes music. His favorite singer is Chris Daughtry.

2 **Match the words to the meanings.**

1. Peru *b*
2. science ____
3. *Heroes* ____
4. Chris Daughtry ____
5. tennis ____
6. Mario Lopez ____

a. a sport
b. a country
c. a school subject
d. a TV star
e. a TV show
f. a singer

3 **Read the article in Part 1 slowly. Circle the words to complete the sentences.**

1. Ms. Rider is a ((basketball)/ soccer) coach.
2. She's a (star / science) teacher.
3. Her (last name / nickname) is Coach R.
4. Rafael is not from (the U.S. / Peru).
5. He likes (music / soccer).
6. His favorite (singer / TV star) is Mario Lopez.

Unit 2 Check Yourself

1 Label the pictures with the words in the box.

☐ actor   ☐ best friend   ☐ model   ☑ soccer coach
☐ basketball player   ☐ cartoon character   ☐ singer   ☐ teacher

1. _soccer coach_

2. _____

3. _____

4. _____

5. _____

6. _____

7. _____

8. _____

2 Write questions.

1. **Q:** _____
   A: I'm eleven.

2. **Q:** _____
   A: She's from Brazil.

3. **Q:** _____
   A: My name is Jeremy.

4. **Q:** _____
   A: He's my science teacher.

5. **Q:** _____
   A: His name is Charlie.

6. **Q:** _____
   A: She's not fifteen. She's seventeen.

3 Choose the correct words to complete the paragraphs.

1. I'm Jack. This is my favorite _cartoon character_
   (cartoon character / soccer player). _____ (His / Her)
   name is Alex, and _____ (she's / her) from Africa.
   _____ (I'm / I'm not) from Africa. I'm from Australia.
   _____ (My / I'm) fifteen. Alex is not fifteen.
   (She's / He's) _____ an adult.

2. I'm Jamie. This is my favorite tennis player.
   _____ (He's / She's) from Spain. _____ (Her / His)
   name is Rafael Nadal. _____ (I'm / He's) from the U.S.
   _____ (I'm not / I'm) from Canada.

What a mess!

1 Check (✓) the items you have in your bag, backpack, or desk.

☐ brush   ☐ notebook

☐ camera   ☐ pen

☐ eraser   ☐ pencil case

☐ hat   ☐ umbrella

2 Write sentences with *This is* or *That's*.

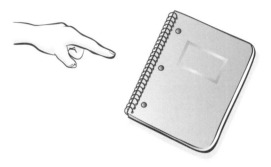

1. (Amy) *This is Amy's backpack.*

2. (Nick) _____

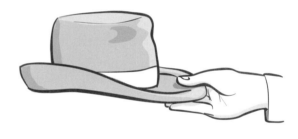

3. (Ricardo) _____

4. (John) _____

5. (Brad) _____

6. (Erica) _____

7. (Ken) _____

8. (Viviana) _____

UNIT 3 Everyday Things

Cool things

1 **Write questions. Then write *a* or *an* to complete the answers.**

1. **Marc** _What's that?_

   Jacki It's _a_ video game.

2. **Marc** _____

   Jacki It's ____ alarm clock.

3. **Jacki** _____

   Marc It's ____ MP3 player.

4. **Marc** _____

   Jacki It's ____ cell phone.

5. **Marc** _____

   Jacki It's ____ laptop.

6. **Jacki** _____

   Marc It's ____ umbrella.

2 **Number the sentences in the correct order.**

1. ____ It's a video game.

   ____ No, it's not. It's a TV.

   ____ Hmm. It's weird. And what's that?

   ____ Wow! It's really cool!

   _1_ Maria, what's this? A desktop computer?

2. ____ No, it's a cell phone. It's a calculator, too.

   ____ It's an MP3 player.

   _1_ What's that, Robby?

   ____ Wow! It's really great.

   ____ Really? It's weird. And what's this? A video game?

1 **What does Kerri say about her things? Write sentences.**

1. _That's my cell phone._   5. _____

2. _____   6. _____

3. _____   7. _____

4. _____   8. _____

2 **Circle the correct words to complete the conversation.**

Mr. Simms Good morning. This is your bag, right?

Kerri Yes. This is (my / your) bag.

Mr. Simms (Who's / What's) this?

Kerri It's (a / an) cell phone.

Mr. Simms Really?

Kerri Yes. It's (a / an) MP3 player, too.

Mr. Simms I see. What's (it / that)?

Kerri Oh, it's (a / an) calculator.

3 **Check (✓) the correct responses.**

1. What's this?
   - ☑ It's a notebook.
   - ☐ Hmm. It's weird.

2. What's that?
   - ☐ Really? It's great!
   - ☐ It's an address book.

3. And what's that?
   - ☐ That's Christina's pen.
   - ☐ Wow! It's really cool.

4. Hey, Carlos. What's this?
   - ☐ What's that? A laptop?
   - ☐ It's Molly's laptop.

Favorite things

1 Complete the puzzle. What's the mystery word?

	¹B	I	C	Y	C	L	E			
²			D			G			D	
³C										
⁴	O			R						
⁵T	S									
	⁶		C							

2 Complete the conversation with *these*, *those*, or *they're*.

Mateo	What are _these_?
Chris	_____ are my favorite trading cards.
Mateo	_____ cool! What are _____?
Chris	_____ are my new T-shirts.
Mateo	_____ nice!

3 Complete the conversations with the sentences in the box.

☐ Hmm. They're very interesting.   ☑ Those are my favorite comic books.
☐ These are my posters.   ☐ What are these?

1. **A** What are those?

   B *Those are my favorite comic books.*

2. **A** _____

   B They're my trading cards.

3. **A** Those are my favorite video games.

   B _____

4. **A** _____

   B Oh, they're nice.

Lesson 12 — Where is it?

1 Look at the picture. Write questions and answers.

1. **Q:** _Where's the umbrella?_

   A: It's next to the dresser.

2. **Q:** _____

   A: They're on the bed.

3. **Q:** _____

   A: It's in the wastebasket.

4. **Q:** Where are the T-shirts?

   A: _____

5. **Q:** Where's the bag?

   A: _____

6. **Q:** Where are the comic books?

   A: _____

2 Choose the correct words to complete the conversation.

Danny Mom! I'm late. _Where's_ (Where's / Where are) my soccer ball?

Mom _____ (It's / They're) under your bed.

Danny OK, but _____ (where's / where are) my books? _____ (It's not / They're not) on my desk.

Mom _____ (It's / They're) on your dresser.

Danny Oh, right. Thanks.
And _____ (where's / where are) my calculator? _____ (It's not / They're not) in my bag.

Mom _____ (It's / They're) on your desk.

1 **Read the blog quickly. Circle the correct answers.**

1. Penny is a (teenager / cat).   2. Stella is a (spider / cat).   3. Stella likes (spiders / cats).

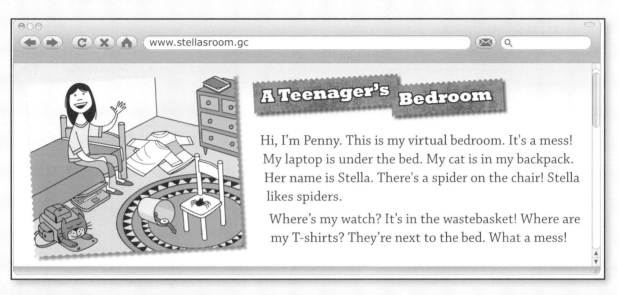

www.stellasroom.gc

A Teenager's Bedroom

Hi, I'm Penny. This is my virtual bedroom. It's a mess! My laptop is under the bed. My cat is in my backpack. Her name is Stella. There's a spider on the chair! Stella likes spiders.

Where's my watch? It's in the wastebasket! Where are my T-shirts? They're next to the bed. What a mess!

2 **Write sentences about the pictures.**

1.

The cat is under the desk.

2.

3.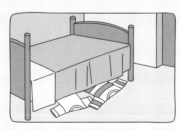

4.

5.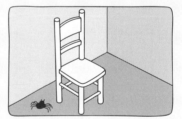

3 **Read the blog in Part 1 slowly. Look at the sentences in Part 2. Make them true for Part 1.**

1. _The laptop is under the bed._

2.

3.

4.

5.

1 Complete the sentences with *a*, *an*, or *the*.

1. What's this? It's ___*a*___ cell phone.

2. That's _____ MP3 player.

3. My books are on _____ laptop.

4. It's _____ alarm clock. It's weird.

5. Jim's bag is next to _____ chair.

6. A What's that? _____ video game?

   B No, it isn't. It's _____ calculator.

2 Look at the picture. Whose things are these? Write Jay's sentences. Begin with *That's*, *This is*, *These are*, or *Those are*.

1. (watch)   *This is my watch.*

2. (pens)   *Those are Cara's pens.*

3. (bicycle)   _____

4. (pencil case)   _____

5. (backpack)   _____

6. (comic books)   _____

7. (erasers)   _____

8. (notebook)   _____

9. (hat)   _____

10. (pencils)   _____

11. (cell phone)   _____

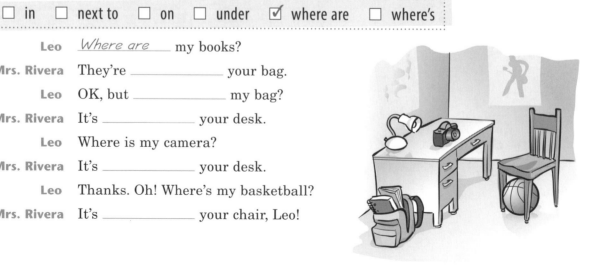

3 Look at the picture. Complete the conversation with the words in the box.

☐ in ☐ next to ☐ on ☐ under ☑ where are ☐ where's

Leo	*Where are* my books?
Mrs. Rivera	They're _____ your bag.
Leo	OK, but _____ my bag?
Mrs. Rivera	It's _____ your desk.
Leo	Where is my camera?
Mrs. Rivera	It's _____ your desk.
Leo	Thanks. Oh! Where's my basketball?
Mrs. Rivera	It's _____ your chair, Leo!

Lesson 13 At the movies

UNIT 4 Around Town

1 Look at the picture. Are the statements true or false?
Check (✓) True or False.

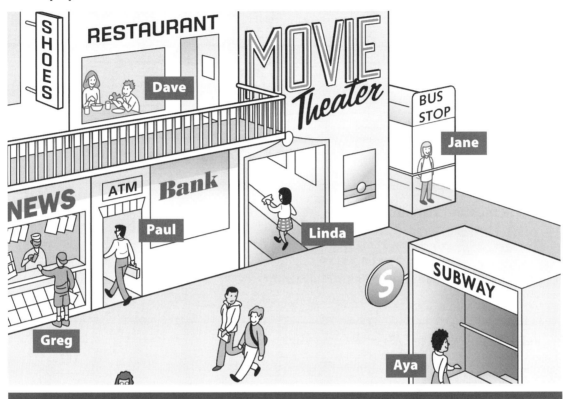

	True	False		True	False
1. Linda is at the movie theater.	✓	☐	4. Greg is at the bank.	☐	☐
2. Paul is at the shoe store.	☐	☐	5. Dave is at the shoe store.	☐	☐
3. Aya is at the subway station.	☐	☐	6. Jane is at the Internet café.	☐	☐

2 Number the sentences in the correct order.

_____ No, I'm not at the theater. I'm at the bus stop.

_____ Well, please hurry. You're late!

_1_ Hi, Carlos. Are you still at home?

_____ OK. I'm sorry.

_____ No, I'm not.

_____ Are you at the movie theater?

3 Complete the conversations.

1. A _Are you 12?_ (12)

   B No, I'm not. I'm 11.

2. A _____ (Mexico City)

   B No, I'm not. I'm from Barcelona.

3. A _____ (soccer player)

   B Yes, I am. It's my favorite sport.

4. A _____ (Salma Hayek fan)

   B Yes, I am. She's my favorite star.

23

Downtown

1 **Look at the picture. Write sentences with the words in the box.**

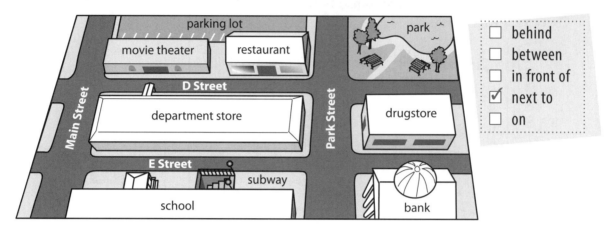

☐ behind
☐ between
☐ in front of
☑ next to
☐ on

1. (movie theater / restaurant)

   The movie theater is next to the restaurant.

2. (parking lot / movie theater and restaurant)

   _____

3. (department store / D Street)

   _____

4. (subway station / school)

   _____

5. (drugstore / park / bank)

   _____

2 **Look at the picture in Part 1. Answer the questions. If the answer is *no*, give the correct information.**

1. Is the movie theater on E Street?

   No, it's not. It's on D Street.

2. Is the department store next to the movie theater?

   _____

3. Is the drugstore between the bank and the department store?

   _____

4. Is the restaurant across from the department store?

   _____

5. Is the parking lot behind the movie theater?

   _____

Mini-review

1 Check (✓) the correct responses.

1. Are you at home?
   - ☑ Yes, I am. I'm in my room.
   - ☐ Yes, it is. It's on Oak Street.

2. Is your school next to a park?
   - ☐ Yes, I am. I'm at school.
   - ☐ No, it isn't. It's across from a park.

3. Are you from Brazil?
   - ☐ Yes, I am. I'm a soccer fan.
   - ☐ No, I'm not. I'm from Peru.

4. Are you 13?
   - ☐ No, I'm not. I'm 14.
   - ☐ Yes, I'm still at the basketball game.

2 Answer the questions in Part 1 with your own information.

1. _____
2. _____
3. _____
4. _____

3 Look at the picture. Then circle the correct words to complete the sentences.

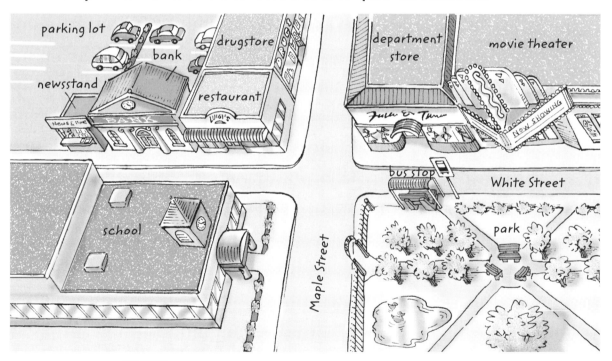

1. The bank is (between / in front of) the newsstand and the restaurant.
2. The drugstore is (behind / on) Maple Street.
3. The bus stop is (across from / in front of) the department store.
4. The movie theater is (next to / between) the department store.
5. The parking lot is (on / behind) the bank.
6. The school is (across from / next to) the park.

At the mall

1 Match the words to make the names of the places. Then write the names of the places.

1. movie __c__   a. rink   _movie theater_
2. bowling ____   b. arcade   _____
3. skating ____   c. theater   _____
4. candy ____   d. alley   _____
5. subway ____   e. store   _____
6. video ____   f. station   _____

2 Write questions and answers.

Hitomi / bus stop

Q: _Is Hitomi at the bus stop?_

A: _No, she's not. She's at the skating rink._

Eric and Kelly / Internet café

Q: _____

A: _____

Kevin / candy store

Q: _____

A: _____

Emily and Maria / video arcade

Q: _____

A: _____

Julia / skating rink

Q: _____

A: _____

Pedro / bookstore

Q: _____

A: _____

Any suggestions?

1 **Look at the pictures. Write sentences using *bored, hot, hungry, thirsty,* or *tired*. Then write a suggestion from the box under each picture.**

1.   _I'm bored._

2.   _____

☐ Go swimming.
☐ Have a sandwich.
☐ Have a soda.
☑ Play volleyball.
☐ Sit down.

Play volleyball.   _____

3.   _____

4.   _____

5.   _____

_____   _____   _____

2 **Number the sentences in the correct order.**

____   Bored? Well, go swimming or play volleyball.

_1_   Hello, Jim. How are you?

____   But I'm tired, too. I'm tired and bored.

____   Oh, hi, Lisa. I'm bored.

____   OK. Go to a movie. There's a good movie at
       the new movie theater.

____   Good idea. Let's go together.

1 Read the blog quickly. Write the ages.

Bored Betty _____ Weather William _____

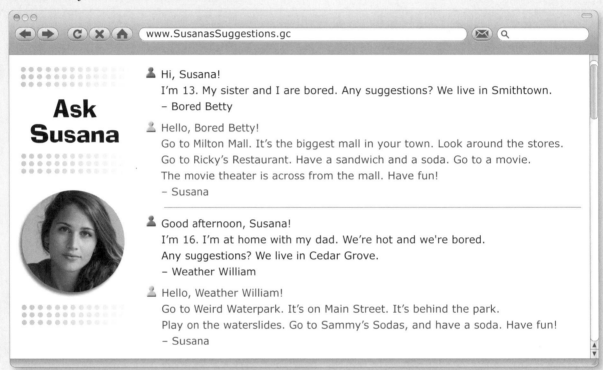

Ask Susana

👤 Hi, Susana!
I'm 13. My sister and I are bored. Any suggestions? We live in Smithtown.
– Bored Betty

👤 Hello, Bored Betty!
Go to Milton Mall. It's the biggest mall in your town. Look around the stores.
Go to Ricky's Restaurant. Have a sandwich and a soda. Go to a movie.
The movie theater is across from the mall. Have fun!
– Susana

👤 Good afternoon, Susana!
I'm 16. I'm at home with my dad. We're hot and we're bored.
Any suggestions? We live in Cedar Grove.
– Weather William

👤 Hello, Weather William!
Go to Weird Waterpark. It's on Main Street. It's behind the park.
Play on the waterslides. Go to Sammy's Sodas, and have a soda. Have fun!
– Susana

2 Complete the letters with the words in the box.

☐ across from   ☐ biggest   ☐ bored   ☑ home   ☐ waterslides

Hi, Susana!
I'm 14. I'm at _____*home*_____ , and I'm _____ . Any suggestions? I live in Lincoln.
– Helen at Home

Hello, Helen at Home!
Go to Freddy's Fun Park with some friends. It's the _____ amusement park there. It's _____ Village Mall. Play paintball or play on the _____ .
Enjoy!
– Susana

3 Read the blog in Part 1 slowly. Check (✓) Betty or William. Sometimes both are possible.

	Betty	William		Betty	William
1. Look around the stores.	✓		4. Go to Ricky's Restaurant.		
2. Go to a movie.			5. Have a soda.		
3. Play on the waterslides.			6. Have fun!		

Check Yourself

1 **Look at the map. Answer the questions with *Yes, it is,* or *No, it's not.***

1. Is the restaurant on Elm Street?

   Yes, it is.

2. Is the parking lot behind the movie theater?

   _____

3. Is the shoe store next to the café?

   _____

4. Is the bank across from the drugstore?

   _____

5. Is the bus stop in front of the bank?

   _____

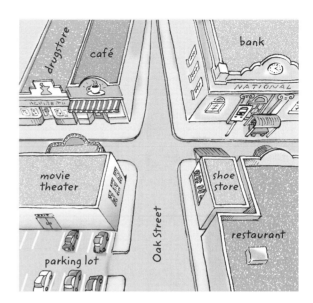

2 **Complete the questions with *Are* or *Is*. Then match the questions to the answers.**

1. *Are* you at home? __d__   a. No, they're not. They're late.
2. _____ the park near the school? _____   b. No, it's not. It's on State Street.
3. _____ Ben and Jill here? _____   c. No, he's not. He's at the movie theater.
4. _____ you hot? _____   d. Yes, I am. I'm in my bedroom.
5. _____ the bank on Main Street? _____   e. Yes, I am. Let's go swimming.
6. _____ James at home? _____   f. Yes, it is. It's next to the school.

3 **Complete the conversations with the sentences in the box.**

☑ I'm bored. ☐ I'm hot. ☐ I'm hungry. ☐ I'm thirsty. ☐ I'm tired.

1. A *I'm bored.*
   B Me, too. Let's play basketball.

2. A _____
   B Have a soda.

3. A _____
   B Let's sit down.

4. A _____
   B Have a sandwich.

5. A _____
   B Me, too. Let's go swimming.

My family

UNIT 5 Family and Home

1 **Look at the picture. Complete the sentences.**

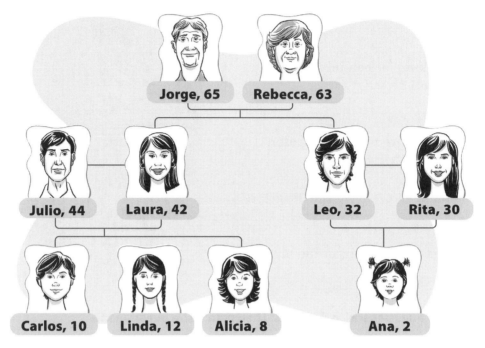

1. Carlos is Linda's ___*brother*___ . He's ___*ten*___ .
2. Leo is Linda's _____ . He's _____ .
3. Rebecca is Linda's _____ . She's _____ .
4. Julio is Linda's _____ . He's _____ .
5. Alicia is Linda's _____ . She's _____ .
6. Laura is Linda's _____ . She's _____ .
7. Ana is Linda's _____ . She's _____ .
8. Rita is Linda's _____ . She's _____ .
9. Jorge is Linda's _____ . He's _____ .

2 **Write sentences about Linda's family. Use *have* or *has*.**

1. Linda's parents / three children
   Linda's parents have three children.

2. Carlos / two sisters
   _____

3. Linda, Carlos, and Alicia / one cousin
   _____

4. Laura / one brother
   _____

5. Linda / one aunt and one uncle
   _____

6. Carlos / no brothers
   _____

7. Alicia / one aunt
   _____

8. Leo / one sister
   _____

9. Linda / one sister and one brother
   _____

10. Ana / no sisters or brothers

Family reunion

1 **Complete the sentences with the words in the boxes.**

1. ☐ smart   ☐ tall

   My cousin is not short. She's _____*tall*_____ .

   My brother is _____*smart*_____ . He likes math and science.

2. ☐ handsome   ☐ pretty

   My father is _____ .

   My Aunt Linda is _____ .

3. ☐ friendly   ☐ shy

   My best friend isn't shy. She's _____ .

   My sister is not crazy. She's very _____ .

2 **Number the sentences in the correct order.**

_____ Mike? He's friendly and very funny.

_____ She's smart. She's shy, too.

__1__ What's her name?

_____ And your brother? What's he like?

_____ Her name is Kayla. She's my sister.

_____ What's she like?

_____ Well, you're friendly and funny, too!

3 **Answer the questions with your own information.**

1. What's your best friend like?

   _____

2. What's your favorite actor like?

   _____

3. What's your math teacher like?

   _____

4. What's your favorite relative like?

   _____

5. What are you like?

   _____

1 Check (✓) the word that is different.

1. ☐ thirty
   ☐ twenty-three
   ☑ friendly

2. ☐ uncle
   ☐ friend
   ☐ sister

3. ☐ hungry
   ☐ handsome
   ☐ pretty

4. ☐ friendly
   ☐ funny
   ☐ cousin

5. ☐ teacher
   ☐ father
   ☐ mother

6. ☐ sixty
   ☐ thin
   ☐ crazy

2 Look at the picture. Write *True* or *False*. Then correct the false statements.

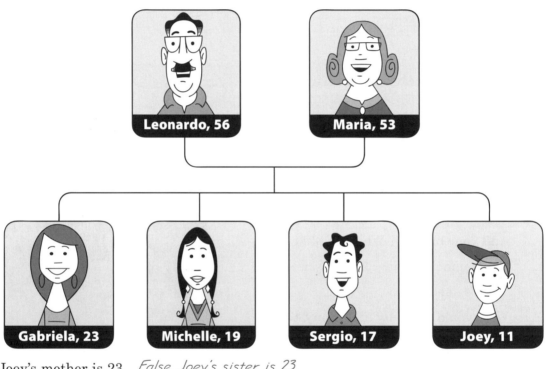

Leonardo, 56   Maria, 53

Gabriela, 23   Michelle, 19   Sergio, 17   Joey, 11

1. Joey's mother is 23. _False. Joey's sister is 23._
2. His father is 56. _____
3. He has three brothers. _____
4. He has two sisters. _____
5. His brother is 10. _____

3 Laura is talking to Nick. Complete her sentences with *have*, *has*, or *'s*.

My name _'s___ Laura. I _____ one brother. He _____ eight, and his name _____ Vincent. He _____ really funny. I _____ a best friend. Her name _____ Julie. Julie _____ a little sister. She _____ only three. Her name _____ Kristen, and she _____ very pretty. Julie _____ a brother, too. He _____ handsome.

My new city

1 **Match the words to the correct pictures.**

1. happy _c_
2. old _____
3. sad _____
4. new _____
5. big _____
6. quiet _____

2 **Complete the sentences with the words in Part 1.**

1. Their neighborhood is noisy. It's not _____ *quiet* _____ .
2. Their school is old. It's not _____ .
3. We're sad. We're not _____ .
4. Our house is small. It's not _____ .

3 **Combine the sentences. Use *they're, we're, their,* or *our*.**

1. You're happy. I'm happy, too.

   We're happy. _____

2. Her neighborhood is quiet. His neighborhood is quiet, too.

   _____

3. He's from Canada. She's from Canada, too.

   _____

4. I'm a little sad. You're a little sad, too.

   _____

5. My school is new. Your school is new, too.

   _____

4 **Circle the correct words to complete the sentences.**

1. (They're /(Their)) school is very nice.
2. We miss Taro, but (our / we're) happy for him.
3. (They're / Our) soccer team is great this year.
4. (Their / We're) last name is Robbins.
5. (They're / Their) from Brazil.
6. (They're / Our) friends are funny.
7. (They're / Their) house isn't big.
8. (We're / Our) teacher is nice.
9. (They're / Their) not from Mexico.
10. (We're / Our) not thirsty.

At home

1 **Match the words in the box to the rooms in the house. Write the numbers.**

> **1** bathroom   **3** dining room   **5** kitchen   **7** yard
> **2** bedroom   **4** garage   **6** living room

2 **Complete the paragraph about the house in Part 1.**
Use *it's* or *it has*.

This is a new house. _It's_ big. _____ in the city, so _____ a small yard. _____ four bedrooms and two bathrooms. _____ a nice kitchen and a big dining room. _____ a living room, too. _____ small, but pretty. _____ a garage. The neighborhood is nice. _____ quiet.

3 **Circle the words that make the sentences true for you.**

1. My home is in the (city / country).

2. It's (old / new).

3. Our neighborhood is (quiet / noisy).

4. Our (house / apartment) has a (big / small) kitchen.

5. It has (one / two / three / four / five) bedrooms.

1 **Read the article quickly. What's the name of Dave and Carol's house?**

_____

Different Houses

A house in a tree!

Greg Sawyer is 12, and his sister, Jessica, is 8. They're children, but they have a house. It's a tree house! It's in the country. It's at their grandparents' house in Kansas. Their tree house has one room. It's a living room with a desk and a few chairs. It's small, but Greg and Jessica think it's great. Greg says, "I'm lucky. My tree house is really awesome!"

A house? A boat? A houseboat!

Dave and Carol Day are from Kentucky. They have a different home. It's a houseboat named Fargo. Their houseboat has a living room, a dining room, a kitchen, a bathroom, and three bedrooms. The Days' children, Alan and Kara, like it a lot. "It's a cool house and a great boat," says Kara.

2 **Complete the sentences with the words in the box.**

☐ awesome	☐ boat	☐ different	☑ lucky

1. My neighborhood has a big mall. I'm really _____*lucky*_____ .

2. We're in _____ math classes. We're not in the same math class.

3. She thinks Zac Efron is _____ . He's her favorite star.

4. His house is in the water. He lives on a _____ .

3 **Read the article in Part 1 slowly. Are these sentences true or false? Check True or False.**

	True	False
1. Greg is 12.	☐	☐
2. Greg has two sisters.	☐	☐
3. The tree house is big.	☐	☐
4. The Days' houseboat has seven rooms.	☐	☐
5. The Days' houseboat is not cool.	☐	☐

1 Answer the questions. Use *it's*, *he's*, *she's*, *they're*, or *I'm* and the words in the box.

☐ big ☐ happy ☐ old ☐ quiet ☑ tall

1. **A** What's your aunt like? Is she short?
   B No, *she's not. She's tall.*

2. **A** What's your school like? Is it small?
   B No, _____

3. **A** What's your brother like? Is he noisy?
   B No, _____

4. **A** What are your CDs like? Are they new?
   B No, _____

5. **A** Are you sad today?
   B No, _____

2 Complete the paragraph with *we*, *our*, *they*, or *their*.

My family and our neighbors are different. ___*Our*___ house is old, and _____ house is new. _____ have a big yard, and _____ have a small yard. But we like _____ house. _____ like their house, too.

3 Complete the sentences. Use *has* or *has no*.

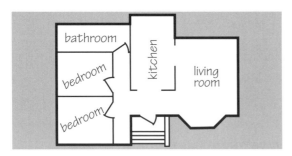

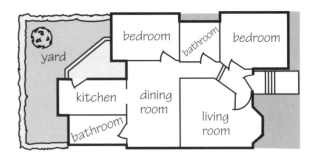

Jane's house

1. ___*It has two*___ bedrooms.
2. _____ dining room.
3. _____ living room.

Tim's house

1. _____ yard.
2. _____ bathrooms.
3. _____ garage.

UNIT 6 At School

1 Complete the crossword puzzle.

Across

Down

B O A R D

2 Complete the sentences with *there's a, there's no, there are,* or *there are no.*

1. *There are* two printers.
2. _____ bookcase.
3. _____ board.
4. _____ screens.
5. _____ scanner.
6. _____ CD/DVD player.
7. _____ remote control.
8. _____ cabinets.

Around school

1 Complete the chart with the words in the box.

☑ auditorium   ☐ cafeteria   ☐ football field   ☐ library   ☐ swimming pool
☐ baseball field   ☐ computer lab   ☐ language lab   ☐ soccer field   ☐ tennis court

Sports facilities	School facilities
	auditorium

2 Circle the correct words to complete the conversation.

Angelo   Rey, your school is cool. (Is / Are) there a gym?

Rey   Yes, there (is / are). There (is / are) three athletic fields, too.

Angelo   (Are / Is) there (a / any) good football players?

Rey   No, there (are / aren't). There (is / are) some good baseball players.

Angelo   Is there (a / any) swimming pool?

Rey   No, there (is / isn't). But there is a cafeteria. It's great!

Angelo   Good. I'm hungry. Let's have a sandwich!

3 Complete the questions with *Is there a* or *Are there any*. Then answer the questions with your own information.

1. *Is there a* _____ swimming pool at your house?

_____

2. _____ media center at your school?

_____

3. _____ athletic fields in your neighborhood?

_____

4. _____ tennis courts on your street?

_____

5. _____ cafeteria at your school?

_____

1 Match the words to make the names of places and things. Then write the names of the places and things.

1. CD/DVD __f__   a. lab   _CD/DVD player_

2. computer ____   b. court   _____

3. tennis ____   c. field   _____

4. athletic ____   d. center   _____

5. remote ____   e. control   _____

6. media ____   f. player   _____

2 Complete the conversations.

1. **A** Are the facilities in your school nice? (Yes)

   B _Yes, they are._ We have great facilities!

2. **A** Are there any tennis courts at your school? (No)

   B _____ But we have three soccer fields.

3. **A** Is there a gym in your school? (Yes)

   B _____ It's next to the library.

4. **A** Are there any new students in your class? (Yes)

   B _____ They're from Puerto Rico.

5. **A** Is there a media center in your school? (No)

   B _____ But there's a new computer lab.

6. **A** Are there any good soccer players in your school? (Yes)

   B _____ Their names are Emily and Hugo.

7. **A** Is there a CD/DVD player in your classroom? (No)

   B _____ But there's a CD/DVD player in the media center.

8. **A** Is there a park near your school? (No)

   B _____ But there's a swimming pool.

3 Answer the questions in Part 2 with your own information.

1. _____   5. _____

2. _____   6. _____

3. _____   7. _____

4. _____   8. _____

Lesson 23 — School subjects

1 **Label the pictures with the words in the box.**

☑ geography ☐ health ☐ history ☐ math ☐ music ☐ science

1.

geography

2.

_____

3.

_____

4.

_____

5.

_____

6.

_____

2 **Complete the paragraph with _on_ or _at_.**

My school schedule is crazy! I have science ___*at*___ 8:30 _____ Monday,
Wednesday, and Friday. I think science is easy. I have math _____ 10:00
every day. Math is difficult. I have music _____ Tuesday and Thursday
_____ 11:00. It's fun. I have computer lab _____ Monday and Wednesday
_____ 1:00. It's my favorite class. I don't like history. I have history every
day _____ 2:00.

3 **Are these statements true or false for you? Write _True_ or _False_. Then correct the false statements.**

1. I have six classes every day.

_____

2. History is my favorite class.

_____

3. I have English on Monday.

_____

4. Art is difficult.

_____

5. I think science is easy.

_____

6. I have math at 10:45 on Monday.

_____

Spring Day

1 Match the two ways to say the same time.

1. It's eight forty-five. _c_
2. It's two fifty. ____
3. It's seven fifteen. ____
4. It's three twenty-five. ____
5. It's twelve forty. ____
6. It's eleven fifty-five ____

a. It's twenty-five after three.
b. It's ten to three.
c. It's a quarter to nine.
d. It's twenty to one.
e. It's five to twelve.
f. It's a quarter after seven.

2 What time is it now? Write the answer two ways.

_____

_____

3 Look at the information on Jake's schedule. Write questions and answers.

8:00
9:00 soccer game – 9:30
10:00
11:00
12:00 lunch – 12:30
1:00 art class – 1:45
2:00
3:00 music class – 3:15
4:00
5:00
6:00
7:00
8:00 movie – 8:00

1. **Q:** _What time is the soccer game?_
   A: It's at nine thirty.

2. **Q:** What time is the movie?
   A: _____

3. **Q:** _____
   A: It's at three fifteen.

4. **Q:** What time is lunch?
   A: _____

5. **Q:** What time is his art class?
   A: _____

4 What time is it now? Write the times.

1. _It's eleven o'clock._

2. _____

3. _____

4. _____

5. _____

6. _____

1 Read the Web site quickly. Underline the times.

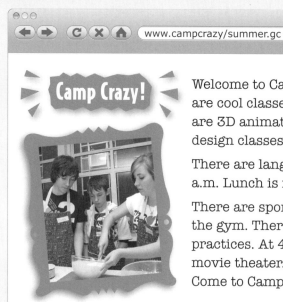

Camp Crazy!

Welcome to Camp Crazy. It's a summer camp. There are cool classes every day. At 10:00 a.m., there are 3D animation classes, juggling classes, fashion design classes, and cooking classes. They're in the gym.

There are language classes in the media center at 11:00 a.m. Lunch is in the cafeteria at 12:00 p.m.

There are sports at 1:30 p.m. on the athletic fields and in the gym. There are soccer, baseball, and basketball team practices. At 4:00 p.m. every day, there is a movie in our movie theater.
Come to Camp Crazy. It's fun!

2 Complete the sentences with the words in the box.

☐ animation ☑ baseball ☐ cooking ☐ summer ☐ fashion

1. I'm on the _____*baseball*_____ team at school.
2. This video game has really cool _____.
3. I have _____ class on Monday. We're making hamburgers.
4. We don't have school in _____.
5. That model knows a lot about _____.

3 Read the Web site in Part 1 slowly. Complete the schedule.

Time	Activity	Place
10:00 a.m.	3D animation, fashion design, and cooking	gym
	language class	media center
12:00 p.m.	lunch	
1:30 p.m.	sports	
	movie	movie theater

Check Yourself

1 Look at the picture. Write questions and answers.

1. (CDs) **Q:** *Are there any CDs?* **A:** *Yes, there are.*
2. (CD/DVD player) **Q:** _____ **A:** _____
3. (computers) **Q:** _____ **A:** _____
4. (printers) **Q:** _____ **A:** _____
5. (remote control) **Q:** _____ **A:** _____
6. (bookcase) **Q:** _____ **A:** _____

2 Look at the picture. Write sentences with *There's a*, *There's no*, *There are*, or *There are no*.

1. (bookcase) *There's no bookcase.*
2. (cabinets) _____
3. (screen) _____
4. (books) _____
5. (chairs) _____
6. (CD/DVD player) _____

3 Write sentences about Gary's schedule.

1. *His English class is at 1:30.*
2. _____
3. _____
4. _____
5. _____
6. _____

GARY'S SCHEDULE

Event
1. English class
1:30
2. history class
8:15
3. music class
Friday
4. health class
Wednesday
5. geography class
10:35
6. science class
11:45

Event

People and countries

1 **Complete the puzzle with seven countries. What's the mystery word?**

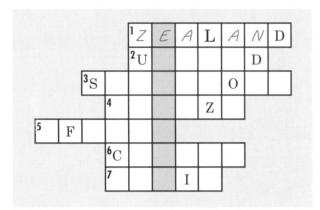

	¹Z	E	A	L	A	N	D
	²U				D		
³S				O			
	4			Z			
5	F						
	⁶C						
	7		I				

1. New _____ is near Australia.

2. Baseball is popular in the _____ States.

3. In _____ , people speak English and Chinese.

4. _____ is small and interesting.

5. People in South _____ speak English, but not American English.

6. The United States is between _____ and Mexico.

7. Delhi is very big city in _____ .

2 **Circle the correct words to complete the conversation.**

Carla You have a lot of friends, José. Are they from Belize?

José No, they (are / aren't). They're from England.

Carla And this girl? (Is / Are) she from England?

José Yes, she (is / isn't). She's great.

Carla This boy is cute. (Is / Are) he from England, too?

José No, he (aren't / isn't). (He's / She's) from Canada. He has six sisters.

Carla Wow!

3 **Complete the questions with *Is* or *Are*. Then answer the questions with your own information.**

1. _____ your city or town in the U.S.? _____

2. _____ you from South Africa? _____

3. _____ your teachers from England? _____

4. _____ your best friend from India? _____

UNIT 7 Around the World

1 **Write the sentences another way.**

1. Susana is from Brazil.

   She's Brazilian.

2. Teresa is from Mexico.

   _____

3. Mike and Tommy are from Australia.

   _____

4. Keiko is from Japan.

   _____

5. James is from England.

   _____

6. Ben and Katy are from the United States.

   _____

2 **Are these statements true or false for you? Check (✓) True or False.**
Then correct the false statements.

	True	False
1. My first language is English.	☐	☑

   My first language isn't English. It's Spanish.

| 2. My parents are from Spain. | ☐ | ☐ |

| 3. My English teacher is Canadian. | ☐ | ☐ |

| 4. My favorite cartoon character is Japanese. | ☐ | ☐ |

| 5. My favorite actor is from Puerto Rico. | ☐ | ☐ |

| 6. My best friend is from Singapore. | ☐ | ☐ |

1 Check (✓) the word that is different.

1. ☐ Peruvian
   ☐ French
   ☑ Japan

2. ☐ England
   ☐ Rio de Janeiro
   ☐ Peru

3. ☐ Australia
   ☐ South Korean
   ☐ Brazil

4. ☐ Japanese
   ☐ Spain
   ☐ Mexican

5. ☐ Brazilian
   ☐ Canada
   ☐ the United States

6. ☐ New Zealand
   ☐ Indian
   ☐ Singapore

2 Complete the paragraph with *is*, *isn't*, *are*, and *aren't*.

My favorite actor ___*is*___ Hugh Jackman. Hugh _____ from Australia. He _____ American, but he _____ a big star in the United States. His movies _____ sad and quiet. They _____ usually action movies. He _____ a very good singer. His musicals _____ very nice. His romantic movies _____ also nice and funny. He _____ really cute.

3 Check (✓) the correct responses.

1. Is he from Vancouver?
   ☑ No, they aren't.
   ☐ Yes, he is.

2. Is Russell Crowe Canadian?
   ☐ Yes, it is.
   ☐ No, he isn't. He's Australian.

3. Are they from France?
   ☐ Yes, they are.
   ☐ Yes, she is.

4. Is she from Japan?
   ☐ No, he isn't. He's from South Korea.
   ☐ Yes, she is. She's a famous singer.

5. Are Marco and Sergio from South Africa?
   ☐ No, they aren't. They're from Brazil.
   ☐ Yes, they are great baseball players.

6. Is Gil de Ferran Brazilian?
   ☐ Yes, he is. He's great.
   ☐ Yes, they are. They're interesting.

1 Circle the correct words to make the sentences true for the United States.

1. Thanksgiving is in (July / (November) / December).

2. Valentine's Day is in (March / May / February).

3. New Year's Eve is in (December / January / February).

4. Independence Day is in (July / June / January).

2 Write the missing months. Complete the series.

1. September	October	_November_	_____
2. March	_____	May	_____
3. _____	February	_____	April
4. June	_____	August	_____
5. _____	March	April	_____
6. _____	_____	December	_____

3 Complete the conversations with the sentences in the box.

☐ It's in February.
☐ It's in May.
☐ It's in October. It's a fun holiday.
☑ It's July. My favorite holiday is Independence Day.
☐ It's New Year's Eve. It's in December.
☐ Yes, it is. It's great.

1. **A** What's your favorite month?
   B _It's July. My favorite holiday is Independence Day._

2. **A** When is Valentine's Day in the U.S.?
   B _____

3. **A** When is Thanksgiving in Canada?
   B _____

4. **A** When is Mother's Day?
   B _____

5. **A** What's your favorite holiday?
   B _____

6. **A** Is Children's Day your favorite holiday?
   B _____

Important days

1 Complete the crossword puzzle with words for these numbers.

Across

5. 18th
6. 24th
8. 1st
9. 3rd
10. 30th

Down

1. 6th
2. 17th
3. 10th
4. 13th
7. 5th

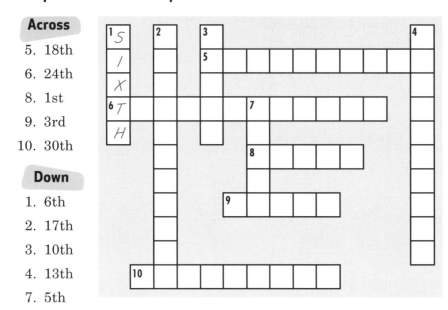

2 Complete the paragraph with *in* or *on*.

Valentine's Day is ___on___ February 14th, Thanksgiving is _____ November, and Christmas is _____ December 25th. But what about Video Game Day? It's _____ September 12th. And Thank You Day? It's _____ September 18th. Here are some good holidays for the family: Sisters' Day is _____ August 4th, Aunts' and Uncles' Day is _____ July 16th, and Family Week is _____ May. But my favorite holiday is _____ September. It's _____ September 4th – that's Teacher's Day!

3 Complete the sentences with *in* or *on* and your own information.

1. My first day of school is _____.

2. My birthday is _____.

3. I'm always happy _____.

4. There are a lot of holidays _____.

1 **Read the article quickly. When is Valentine's Day in Brazil?**

_____

❤ Valentine's Day Around the World ❤

Valentine's Day is on February 14th in many countries – the United States, Canada, India, England, and Peru. In Peru, the name for Valentine's Day is the Day of Love and Friendship. In Brazil, Valentine's Day is on June 12th.

On Valentine's Day in the United States, many boys give girls flowers. In South Korea and Japan on this day, girls give boys chocolate or candy. Then on March 14th – on White Day – boys give girls chocolate or candy.

When is Valentine's Day in your country? Is it a fun holiday?

2 **Choose the correct word to complete the sentences.**

1. Let's have a (celebration / holiday) for my birthday.

2. It's an (important / August) holiday in the U.S., Mexico, and other countries.

3. People (receive / chocolate) gifts on their birthdays.

4. New Year's Eve is a big (month / holiday) in many countries.

3 **Read the article in Part 1 slowly. Then answer the questions.**

1. Is Valentine's Day on February 14th in Canada? _Yes, it is._

2. Is The Day of Love and Friendship a celebration in the U.S.? _____

3. Is Valentine's Day on June 12th in Peru? _____

4. Is White Day a celebration in Japan and South Korea? _____

1 Complete the conversation with *is*, *isn't*, *are*, or *aren't*.

Lee   Hey, Deb. Look at all of my CDs.

Deb   Wow! You have a lot of CDs.

Lee   Yes, and this _____ my favorite CD. This _____ Luciana Mello. She's my favorite singer.

Deb   _____ she famous?

Lee   No, she _____ . But she's great.

Deb   _____ all your favorite singers Brazilian?

Lee   No, they _____ . I like American singers, too.

2 Write questions.

1. A (England) *Is he from England?* _____
   B Yes, he is. He's British.

2. A (Peruvian) _____
   B No, they aren't. Tia and Marie are Colombian.

3. A (April) _____
   B No, it isn't. Mother's Day is in May.

4. A (good) _____
   B Yes, they are. The Orioles are a good baseball team!

5. A (Brazil) _____
   B No, he isn't. He's from Puerto Rico.

3 Write sentences about people's birthdays.

	Month	Day
1. Sebastian	9	5
2. Shannon	2	
3. Mr. Brock	12	21
4. Paco	4	11
5. Kelly	8	

1. *Sebastian's birthday is on September 5th.*
2. *Shannon's birthday is in . . .*
3. _____
4. _____
5. _____

4 Write the words.

1. 14th _____ *fourteenth* _____   4. 9th _____
2. 4th _____   5. 16th _____
3. 23rd _____   6. 22nd _____

Favorite places

1 Circle the correct words to complete the sentences.

1. My favorite store is Hip-Hop Clothes. There are cool clothes in the store, and it's always (**crowded** / quiet).

2. There are a lot of museums, parks, and restaurants in London.
   It's (cute / exciting). It isn't (boring / happy).

3. The beach is my favorite place for a vacation. There aren't a lot of stores at the beach, and it's (beautiful / noisy).

4. The city zoo has lots of animals. It's (fun / old), and the animals are cute.

5. The Getty Museum in Los Angeles isn't (boring / crazy). You can learn a lot there. It's very (small / interesting).

2 Complete the conversation with the sentences in the box.

☐ It's really interesting.	☐ What's your favorite place in Florida, Steve?
☐ It's the Kennedy Space Center.	☑ What's your favorite place in Florida, Talisa?
☐ What's it like?	

Steve *What's your favorite place in Florida, Talisa?*

Talisa It's Disney World.

Steve _____

Talisa It's exciting. There are a lot of fun things there. There are cartoon characters, stores, and restaurants.

Steve Wow! That's great.

Talisa _____

Steve _____

Talisa What's it like?

Steve _____

1 Write the words in the correct column.

☑ dance ☐ draw ☐ Ping-Pong ☐ sing ☐ skateboard ☐ the guitar

I can . . .	I can play . . .
dance.	

2 Number the sentences in the correct order.

_____ Great! I can sing. Let's enter.

_____ Can Mary sing?

_____ No. I can't dance at all. But I can play the guitar.

_____ You and me? Good idea!

__1__ It's a talent show. Hey! There's Mary's name.

_____ No, she can't. But she can dance.

_____ Can you dance?

3 Look at the pictures. Write questions and answers.

❶

Q: _Can he sing?_
A: _No, he can't._

❷

Q: _____
A: _____

❸

Q: _____
A: _____

❹

Q: _____
A: _____

4 Write sentences about yourself. Use *I can* and *I can't.*

1. _____

2. _____

3. _____

4. _____

Mini-review

1 **Answer the questions with the information in the chart.**

	Ethan	Brenda
sing	☐	☑
draw	☑	☑
play the guitar	☑	☐
dance	☐	☑

1. Can Brenda play the guitar? _No, she can't._

2. Can Ethan draw? _____

3. Can Brenda dance? _____

4. Can Ethan sing? _____

5. Can Brenda draw? _____

6. Can Ethan dance? _____

2 **Complete the questions with *What's* or *Can*. Then answer the questions.**

1. _What's_ your English class like?

_____

2. _____ your math class like?

_____

3. _____ your best friend skateboard?

_____

4. _____ your favorite city like?

_____

5. _____ you speak Spanish?

_____

6. _____ your teacher play the guitar?

_____

3 **Complete conversation 1. Then complete conversation 2 with your own information.**

1. **A** What's your favorite place in Puerto Rico?

   B _It's Old San Juan._ (Old San Juan)

   A What's it like?

   B _____ (beautiful / interesting)

2. **A** _____ in your town?

   B _____

   A What's it like?

   B _____

School fashion

1 Label the clothes with the words in the box.

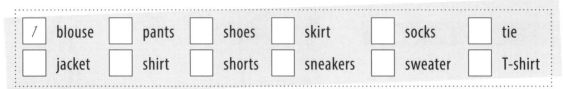

1	blouse		pants		shoes		skirt		socks		tie
	jacket		shirt		shorts		sneakers		sweater		T-shirt

TARA   TAKESHI   MARK

2 Write questions.

❶

What color are the shorts?

They're blue.

❷

They're green and white.

❸
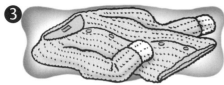

It's green.

❹

They're brown.

❺

It's blue and red.

❻
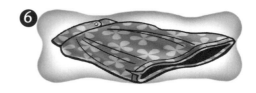

It's pink and purple.

Teen tastes

1 **Write each conversation in the correct order.**

1. ☐ Oh, I don't like rap music. I like pop music.

   ☐ It's my new rap CD. My favorite music is rap.

   ☑ What's this?

   A *What's this?*

   B _____

   A _____

2. ☐ I like pop music, too. But my favorite music is classical.

   ☐ I like pop music. What about you, Amy?

   ☐ That's great! I like classical music, too.

   A _____

   B _____

   A _____

2 **Are these statements true or false for you? Check (✓) True or False. Then correct the false statements.**

	True	False
1. I don't like comic books. I think they're boring.	☐	☑
I love comic books. They're cool.		
2. I love classical music. It's beautiful.	☐	☐
3. I don't like basketball. I think it's difficult.	☐	☐
4. I like science. It's easy for me.	☐	☐
5. I don't like music stores. They're too noisy!	☐	☐

1 Read the Web site quickly. When is the city fair?

_____

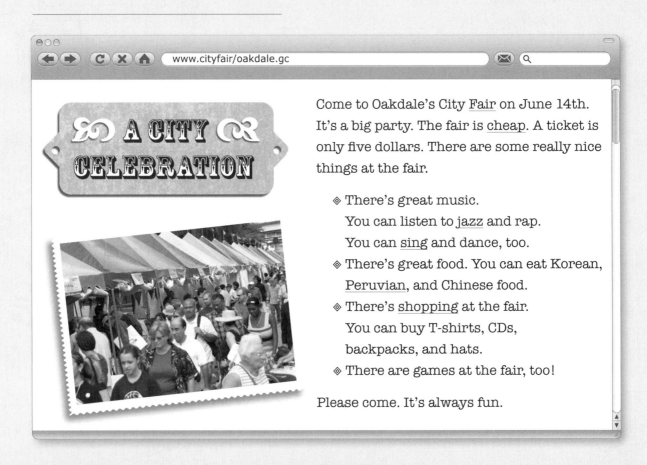

Come to Oakdale's City <u>Fair</u> on June 14th. It's a big party. The fair is <u>cheap</u>. A ticket is only five dollars. There are some really nice things at the fair.

◈ There's great music.
  You can listen to <u>jazz</u> and rap.
  You can <u>sing</u> and dance, too.
◈ There's great food. You can eat Korean, <u>Peruvian</u>, and Chinese food.
◈ There's <u>shopping</u> at the fair.
  You can buy T-shirts, CDs, backpacks, and hats.
◈ There are games at the fair, too!

Please come. It's always fun.

2 Complete the paragraph with the underlined words from Part 1.

This street ____*fair*____ is awesome. You can listen to _____. You can _____ songs, too. You can even eat _____ food! The _____ is great. The T-shirts are only six dollars! They're _____.

3 Read the Web site in Part 1 slowly. Write _True_ or _False_. Then correct the false statements.

1. The city fair is in Pineville. _False. It's in Oakdale._
2. The fair is in October. _____
3. The city fair is a big party. _____
4. The fair is cheap. _____
5. There's rock music at the fair. _____
6. You can play games at the fair. _____

Unit 8   Check Yourself

1 Complete the conversations with the questions in the box.

☐ What color are your shoes?   ☐ What's the zoo like?
☐ What color is your cell phone?   ☑ What's your school like?

1. **A** *What's your school like?*

   B It's crowded. It has a lot of students.

2. **A** _____

   B It's pink. It's really cute!

3. **A** _____

   B It's interesting. There are a lot of animals.

4. **A** _____

   B They're blue. They're old, too.

2 Match the questions to the answers.

1. What's your favorite food? _e_
2. What's your favorite school subject? ____
3. What's your math class like? ____
4. What's the museum like? ____
5. What's your favorite music? ____
6. What's your soccer coach like? ____

   a. Rap. It's really cool!
   b. She's nice. And she can play very well!
   c. It's boring. I don't like math.
   d. I like science. It's fun.
   e. Italian. I love pizza!
   f. It's crowded, but very interesting.

3 Complete the paragraph with *can, can't, like, love,* or *don't like*.

    My favorite place in Sydney is Bondi Beach. It's very exciting and interesting. I *don't like* boring places. I _____ the water and the sun. I _____ swim very well, too. My brother _____ swim. But he _____ skateboard! So Bondi Beach is his favorite place, too.

Check Yourself 57

Illustration Credits

Adolar Mendes 22, 37, 40, 41, 43, 50

Michael Brennan 6, 20 (*top*), 23, 34, 43 (*bottom*)

Andrea Champlin 16, 24

Laurie Conley 7, 13, 18 (*bottom*), 19 (*top*), 27, 48

David Coulson 12, 22, 26

Bruce Day 2, 29 (*bottom*), 44, 48

Adam Hurwitz 36 (*bottom*)

Larry Jones 3, 8, 36 (*top*), 39, 52, 54

Marcelo Pacheco 7, 17, 20 (*bottom*), 21, 27, 32, 55

Félix Reiners 5, 9, 18, 19, 30, 31

Andrew Schiff 25, 29 (*top*)

Sattu Rodrigues 19

Photo Acknowledgements

The authors and publishers acknowledge the following sources of copyright material and are grateful for the permissions granted. While every effort has been made, it has not always been possible to identify the sources of all the material used, or to trace all copyright holders. If any omissions are brought to our notice, we will be happy to include the appropriate acknowledgements on reprinting.

Workbook

p.2: ©Peter Griffith/Masterfile; p.3 (1): ©Steve Prezant/Masterfile; p.3 (2): ©Blend Images/Shutterstock; p.3 (3): ©RAW FILE/Masterfile; p. 3 (4): ©Jack Wild/Taxi Japan/Getty Images; p.4 (T): ©Elizabeth Knox/Masterfile; p.4 (B): ©Keith Brofsky/UpperCut Images/Getty Images Plus/Getty Images; p.7 (small dog): ©Erik Lam/Shutterstock; p.7 (large dog): ©Artiga Photo/Corbis; p.7 (girl+dog): ©Stockbyte/Getty Images; p.10 (T): Steve Granitz/WireImage; p.10 (TC): ©Andrew Kent/Corbis; p.10 (C): ©Jim Spellman/WireImage/Getty Images; p.10 (BC): ©Shirlaine Forrest/Getty Images for MTV; p.10 (B): ©ILLUMINATION ENTERTAINMENT/THE KOBAL COLLECTION; p.11 (TL): ©David Young-Wolff/The Image Bank/Getty Images; p.11 (TR): ©Hilary Brodey/Photodisc/Getty Images; p.11 (BL): ©Albert L. Ortega/Getty Images; p.11 (BR): ©Jaroslaw Wojcik/Getty Images; P.13: ©Kali Nine LLC/iStock/Getty Images Plus; P.14 (L): ©2/Inti St. Clair/Ocean/Corbis; P.14 (R): ©Camille Tokerud/Photodisc/Getty Images; P.15 (1): ©SuperstudioThe Image Bank/Getty Images; P.15 (2): ©Mike Marsland/WireImage/Getty Images; P.15 (3): ©John Schults/ZUMA/Corbis; P.15 (4): ©DreamPictures/Blend Images/Getty Images; P.15 (5): ©Jesse D. Garrabrant/NBAE via Getty Images; P.15 (6): ©l i g h t p o e t/Shutterstock; P.15 (7): ©ILLUMINATION ENTERTAINMENT/THE KOBAL COLLECTION; P.15 (8): ©Anton Oparin/Shutterstock; P.15 (Adventure Time): ©Cartoon Network/Everett/ REX; p.15 (Nadal): ©DOMINIQUE FAGET/AFP/Getty Images; p.19 (1): ©Mindscape studio/Shutterstock; p.19 (2): ©Jeff Blackler/REX; p.19 (3): ©Hulton Archive/Getty Images; p.19 (4): ©COLUMBIA PICTURES / THE KOBAL COLLECTION; p.19 (5 red): ©GaryAlvis/E+/Getty Images; p.19 (5 blue): ©clu/iStock / Getty Images Plus/Getty Images; p.19 (6): ©Anthony Berenyi/Shutterstock; p.23: ©KL Services/Masterfile/Corbis; p.27: ©Vikram Raghuvanshi/iStock / Getty Images Plus/Getty Images; p.28: ©Ariel Skelley/Blend Images/Getty Images; p.33 (a): ©Nathan Griffith/Alamy; p.33 (b): ©Jose Luis Pelaez, Inc./Blend Images/Corbis; p.33 (c): ©SW Productions/ Stockbyte/Getty Images; p.33 (d): ©Tom Le Goff/Photodisc/Getty Images; p.33 (e): ©Robert Churchill/E+/Getty Images; p.33 (f): ©Johan Swanepoel/Shutterstock; p.33 (C "busy"): ©Sergiu Turcanu / Alamy; p.33 (B: "quiet"): ©William Manning / Alamy; p.35 (T): ©Paul Bradforth/Alamy; p.35 (B): ©Scott Leigh/iStock/Getty Images Plus/ Getty Images; p.37 (3): ©Meiko Arquillos/UpperCut Images/Getty Images; p.37 (4): ©Finnbarr Webster/Alamy; p.37 (6): ©Hugh Threlfall/Alamy; p.37 (1): ©Dragan/Shutterstock; p.37 (2): ©Suzanne Tucker/Shutterstock; p.37 (3): ©Catapult/Getty Images; p.37 (5): ©Aaron Amat/Shutterstock; p.38 (T): David Schmidt/Masterfile; p.38 (B): ©ClassicStock /Alamy; p.42: ©Brian Mitchell/Corbis; p.45(1): Karin Dreyer/Blend Images/Getty Images; p.45(2): ©Denis Kuvaev/Shutterstock; p.45(3): ©Andreas Pollok/The Image Bank/Getty Images; p.45(4): ©DAJ/Getty Images; p.45(5): ©Michael Prince/Corbis; p.45(6): ©Toby Burrows/Photodisc/Getty Images; p.46 (L): ©Walter McBride/WireImage/Getty Images; p.46 (R): ©20TH CENTURY FOX / THE KOBAL COLLECTION / HAYES, KERRY; p.47: ©Ron Stroud/Masterfile; p.49: ©Datacraft Co Ltd; p.50: ©racorn/Shutterstock; p.51 (L): ©James Randklev/Photographer's Choice RF/Getty Images; p.51 (R): ©NASA - digital version copyright Science Faction/ Getty Images; p.53 (TL): ©Jake Hellbach/Alamy; p.53 (TR): ©Jason Lugo/E+/Getty Images; p.53 (B): ©Richard Cummins/Robert Harding World Imagery/Getty Images; p.56: ©Jeff Greenberg / Alamy; p.57 (T): ©Monkey Business Images/Monkey Business/Corbis; p.57 (BL): ©Dave G. Houser/Corbis; p.57 (BL): ©Paul A. Souders/Corbis

Cover photograph by Joe McBride/Getty Images.

Notes

Notes

Notes

Notes